# NOVENA
## TO THE
# HOLY SPIRIT

by Fr. Philip G. Bochanski

*All booklets are published thanks to the
generous support of the members of the
Catholic Truth Society*

## CATHOLIC TRUTH SOCIETY
PUBLISHERS TO THE HOLY SEE

# Contents

# ───── Praying to the Holy Spirit ─────

## The Fruits of the Holy Spirit

Gathered with his Apostles in the Upper Room, Jesus reminded them that he had chosen and appointed them to "go and bear fruit that will remain" (*John* 15:16). At that same Last Supper, he promised them that they would not be alone in accomplishing this mission: "I will ask the Father," he said, "and he will give you another Advocate to be with you always, the Spirit" (*John* 14:16-17). The story of the early church related in the Acts of the Apostles shows just how Jesus kept his promise: the Holy Spirit descended on the Apostles at Pentecost, and they went out to accomplish great things in the mission of evangelising the world.

Although we have all heard of the Holy Spirit, he can sometimes be the most difficult of the three Persons of the Trinity to understand. Jesus himself compares the Holy Spirit to the wind: we cannot see the wind, which is invisible, but we recognise it because we can feel it blowing on our skin, and we can see its effects on the objects around us. In the same way, although the Spirit himself is invisible, and often works in hidden ways, we can recognise his presence in the works that he accomplishes in those who believe. St Paul calls these works - "love, joy, peace, patience, kindness, generosity, faithfulness, gentleness, self-control" - the fruits of the Spirit (*Galatians* 5:22-23).

In the *Summa Theologica* (I-II, Q. 70), St Thomas Aquinas explains that these spiritual qualities in a person are called "fruits" because they are the result of one's cooperation with the Holy Spirit. They are different from the theological virtues (faith, hope and love) and the gifts of the Holy Spirit (wisdom, knowledge, understanding, counsel, fortitude, piety and holy fear), which are infused, that is, poured into the heart directly by God. Rather, the fruits of the Spirit come about in the soul when we receive the virtues and gifts of the Spirit, and let them change the way we live; in other words, when we put them into practise. The gifts are graces: purely the initiative of God, the giver of all good gifts. The fruits are evidence of our response to God's gift. They combine our own efforts with the Spirit of God working in us, and show the world the power of God at work in our lives.

### The Novena to the Holy Spirit

Before he ascended into heaven, Jesus instructed the apostles to remain in Jerusalem and to pray for the coming of the Holy Spirit. If we wish to receive the power of the Holy Spirit that will help us to bear his fruits, we too must follow this command and example of fervent prayer.

Because there were nine days between that first Ascension Thursday and Pentecost Sunday, the Church has developed the practise of the *novena* devotion, a set of prayers and meditations that is repeated every day for nine days to pray for a special intention (the Latin word for "nine" is *novem*). The Catholic faithful pray novenas to prepare for the feasts of the liturgical year, to express devotion to the Blessed Mother or a particular saint, or in times of special need. This repetition of prayers for nine days has nothing to do with superstition or some sort of "magic number". Rather, it is a way for us to connect ourselves with the example of the Apostles, who were obedient to Christ's command to make the "original" novena.

The rest of this booklet contains prayers and devotions that may be used to make a novena of prayers to the Holy Spirit, seeking help that we may bear his fruits. Certainly, a good time to pray such a novena would be on the nine days between Ascension and Pentecost, but there are many other reasons to pray for the Spirit's fruits during the whole year. A new job, a new school year, a move to a new location, are all good times to pray for the guidance and support of the Advocate that Jesus promised to his disciples. Or perhaps we have recognised that peace, love, joy, or some of the other fruits are missing from our lives. Prayer for the action of the

Holy Spirit is the necessary first step if these fruits are to grow in our lives. Whatever the reason, we can be sure that the Holy Spirit hears our prayers, and will pour out his graces on us so that we can bear fruit in abundance.

### The Vessel of the Holy Spirit

When the Apostles made the original novena to the Holy Spirit, they were not alone. In the Upper Room, they "devoted themselves with one accord to prayer, together with some women, and Mary the mother of Jesus, and his brothers" (*Acts* 1:14). Because we belong to the Communion of Saints, we too can be sure that as we pray, we are in the company of the Blessed Mother and the Apostles, as well as myriads of saints from every time and place. In our meditations during this novena, we will pay particular attention to one saint, a sixteenth-century Roman priest who has come to be known as the "vessel of the Holy Spirit."

Around the year 1533, a young man from Florence entered the gates of the city of Rome, drawn there by a special attraction, what he perceived to be a call from God himself. He soon found employment as a tutor to the two sons of a fellow Florentine who was director of the custom-house - a job that provided him with a roof and a bed, food and drink, and a great deal of free time, which he put to good use.

Sometimes he would go to volunteer in the hospitals, and often he would spend long hours in prayer in one of Rome's many churches. Nearly every day he would walk around the city, seeking out young men like himself who also had time on their hands, and striking up conversations with them.

From this humble beginning, Philip Romolo Neri built a lifestyle and a ministry that would lead to his being called "The Second Apostle of Rome". For out of the friendships he made in these early days would come his own vocation to the priesthood, and the gathering of a community of lay people for prayers and fellowship each afternoon in a chapel - also called an "oratory" - above the aisle of his church of San Girolamo della Carità. Soon these afternoon exercises became known as "The Oratory", and gave a name also to the congregation of priests and brothers that was established to conduct them. Through it all, Philip Neri had an impact on thousands of people - paupers and popes, men and women of every class and career - over a lifetime of eighty years. Everyone agreed that there was something special about this humble, unassuming man, which drew people to him "as the magnet draws iron."

### Heart of Fire

To depict this special quality that people experienced in their contact with him, St Philip is often described in art, poetry and prayers as having a heart of fire. But this is not merely a metaphor. During his lifetime many people noticed that he seemed always to be warm; he was often flushed, and would walk around with his cassock unbuttoned at the chest, even in the middle of winter. Not only that, but several of his disciples reported that his heart used to beat violently when he prayed or preached, sometimes enough to shake the bench on which he was sitting. Some people could hear his heart beating across the room, and others experienced unspeakable peace and joy when he embraced them and held their heads to his breast. Typical of St Philip, although so many people witnessed this incredible warmth and palpitation of his heart, no one knew where it came from, until St Philip was on his deathbed. There he told one of his favorite disciples, Pietro Consolini, who waited until he himself lay dying, in 1643, before he revealed the secret of St Philip's personal Pentecost.

Over a period of about ten years, while St Philip was in his twenties and still a layman, he used to spend many nights in prayer, either on the porticos of Roman churches, or in the catacombs, the underground burial places of the martyrs outside the walls of the city. On the vigil of Pentecost in 1544, St Philip was praying in the Catacombs of St Sebastian, on the Via Appia, as he had done many times, and asking God to give him the Holy Spirit. As the night passed, St Philip was suddenly filled with great joy, and had a vision of the Holy Spirit, who appeared to him as a ball of fire. This fire entered into St Philip's mouth, and descended to his heart, causing it to expand to twice its normal size, and breaking two of his ribs in the process. He said that it filled his whole body with such joy and consolation that he finally had to throw himself on the ground and cry out, "No more, Lord! No more!"

This mystical experience was a defining moment in St Philip's life. But he did not make much of its extraordinary nature, and he would not want us to do so either. "As for those who run after visions," he would say, "we must lay hold of them by the feet and pull them to the ground by force, lest they should fall into the devil's net." Rather, its importance lay in the fact that, from that moment on, St Philip was convinced and constantly aware of the presence and action of the Holy Spirit in him and through him. This mystical experience of the Spirit gave him great confidence in living his vocation, and carrying out what he saw to be his special mission. He was sure that he had received the gifts of the Holy Spirit, and this assurance set him free to bear the Spirit's fruits.

The world in which we live today is not terribly different from the materialistic, self-centered, overly sensual Rome that St Philip evangelised in the sixteenth century. He was a driving force for renewal in his own day, and his example and advice are as relevant and necessary in our day as they were in his. Above all, St Philip shines forth as a sign of hope - of the great things that become possible when a person cooperates with the power of the Holy Spirit working in him, and dedicates himself to bearing spiritual fruit. The saint of gentleness and kindness, who practised perfect chastity and tireless generosity, is an example of patience who draws us to celebrate the peace, joy and love that come from the presence and work of the Holy Spirit in each human heart. Let us pray with him for an outpouring of the same Holy Spirit that set his heart on fire, that we may imitate him in bearing the fruits of the Spirit.

## Day One

# Love

**Hymn**
(*May be chosen from pp. 48-52*)

**Antiphon**
Come, Holy Spirit, fill the hearts of your faithful, and kindle in them the fire of your love. Send forth your Spirit, and they will be created,
- And you will renew the face of the earth.

**Prayer**
God our Father, your love for us gives us strength to accomplish your will. Fill us, as you filled St Philip, with the love of your Holy Spirit, so that like him we may share your love with others. We ask this through Christ our Lord. Amen.

**Reading** (1 *John* 4:7-9)
Beloved, let us love one another, because love is of God; everyone who loves is begotten by God and knows God. Whoever is without love does not know God, for God is love. In this way the love of God was revealed to us: God sent his only son into the world so that we might have life through him.

**Responsory**                    (cf. *Romans* 5:5; 8:11)

The love of God has been poured into our hearts (alleluia).

- By his Spirit living in us, (alleluia).

**Meditation**

> *I love, and loving must love ceaselessly,*
> *So whole a conquest in me love hath won;*
> *My love to Thee, Thy love to me dost run;*
> *In Thee I live, and Thou dost live in me.*

These words, from one of the two sonnets that survive from St Philip, summarise well the way that he experienced and understood the love of God and neighbour. "We must give ourselves to God altogether," he insisted, for God has already given himself completely to us. As St Thomas says, in the fruit of love "the Holy Spirit is given in a special manner, as in His own likeness, since He Himself is love." Such a total gift of self on God's part demands a response that is likewise total, and leaves no room for any rival. "As much love as we give to creatures," St Philip says, "just so much do we take from the Creator."

Yet he will insist over and over that the fruit of our love for God must be visible in the love we have for our neighbours, and in our concern for them in their need: "God never comes where there is no love of neighbour." From the very beginning of his days in Rome, long before his ordination as a priest, and even before his Pentecost, St Philip organized charitable groups and institutions in the city. Later, during the Holy Year of 1550, he established the Confraternity of the Holy Trinity (*Santissima Trinità dei Pellegrini*) to serve the pilgrims who came to Rome for the Jubilee. This work continued in subsequent Holy Years, and in the interim the confraternity devoted itself to caring for the sick in hospitals and convalescent homes. St Philip frequently joined in their work, even in his old age, and constantly sent his penitents to the hospitals as well. "A diligent charity in ministering to the sick," he advised them, "is a compendious way to the acquisition of perfect virtue."

This was dirty, exhausting, thankless work, but he performed it with cheerfulness and an evident love - and expected his disciples to come to it with the same attitude. Many found it a great mortification, especially those who in their own lives were used to being cared for and waited on, rather than the other way around. But this mortification of self-will and pride is at the heart of St Philip's spiritual approach, and was for him the measure of all spiritual progress: "The greatness of our love for God must be tested by the desire we have of suffering for His love." He was not oblivious to the sacrifices that works of charity involved, but he knew that real charity would overcome these obstacles. "The love of God makes us do great things."

**Litany**
(*Optional; may be chosen from pp. 53-60*)
**Our Father, Hail Mary, Glory be.**

**Concluding Prayer**
Heavenly Father, hear the prayers that we make in the name of your Son, and give us the Paraclete whom he promised you would send. May your love for us give us strength to respond to you, and to bear fruit in our love for you and for our neighbour. We ask this through Christ our Lord. Amen.

# Day Two

# Joy

**Hymn**
(*May be chosen from pp. 48-52*)

**Antiphon**
Come, Holy Spirit, fill the hearts of your faithful, and kindle in them the fire of your love. Send forth your Spirit, and they will be created,
- And you will renew the face of the earth.

**Prayer**
Father, the presence of your Holy Spirit gives joy to your people. Open our hearts to receive your Spirit, that like St Philip we may rejoice in his presence every day of our lives. We ask this through Christ our Lord. Amen.

**Reading** (1 *Peter* 1:8-9)
Although you have never seen [Christ] you love him; even though you do not see him now you believe in him, you rejoice with an indescribable and glorious joy, as you attain the goal of your faith, the salvation of your souls.

**Responsory**                    (cf. *Romans* 5:5; 8:11)

The love of God has been poured into our hearts (alleluia).

- By his Spirit living in us, (alleluia).

## Meditation

"The necessary result of the love of charity is joy: because every lover rejoices at being united to the beloved." So teaches St Thomas, and this fruit of the Spirit was so evident in the life of St Philip that it has become almost synonymous with his name. "Light of Holy Joy" Cardinal Newman calls him, and a contemporary author who wrote a philosophical treatise on the subject titled it simply "Philip: Or Christian Joy". Many eyewitness accounts give testimony to the great spiritual joy that seemed to overflow from St Philip's heart, and was evident to everyone who met him.

Often times this joy would have physical manifestations: some witnesses report seeing St Philip levitate at the altar while saying Mass, and the servers who assisted at his Mass later in his life tell us that, when he came to the elevation of the Host before Communion, he would sometimes be lost in contemplation for hours at a time. People who came to his room early in the morning for confession often found him lost in prayer, perhaps standing in the middle of the room with his shirt half-buttoned, so distracted by love and joy that he had forgotten what he was doing.

We have seen already, though, that St Philip did not put much stock in these ecstatic gifts and manifestations in his own life, and he positively discouraged them in others. "He who desires ecstasies and visions does not know what he is desiring," he would say, and he meant it. The raptures that used to come upon him while he was preaching or celebrating Mass were a source of great embarrassment and distress for him, and he would do anything he could think of to distract himself so that his emotions did not overpower him. With others he was equally cautious. "Philip did not make much account of this warmth and acuteness of feeling, for he said that emotion was not devotion, that tears were no sign that a man was in the grace of God; neither must we suppose a man holy merely because he weeps when he speaks of religion."

Still, the holy joy that filled St Philip's heart was difficult to hide, and in many cases was positively contagious. "What St Paul says of himself seemed to be fulfilled in Philip," Newman tells us, quoting the second letter to the Corinthians: "I am filled with consolation - I over-abound with joy." His penitents often felt joyful simply being in his room, even if he were not there, and some who were in distress only needed to stand at the door of his room, without going in, to feel better. Though some people are naturally outgoing and expressive, it seems that this was not the case with St Philip, and he was always ready to attribute the joy he felt and shared with others to its real source. "The Holy Spirit is the master of prayer and causes us to abide in continual peace and cheerfulness, which is a foretaste of Paradise. We ought to pray God fervently to increase in us every day the light and heat of his goodness."

### Litany
(*Optional; may be chosen from pp. 53-60*)
**Our Father, Hail Mary, Glory be.**

### Concluding Prayer
Heavenly Father, hear the prayers that we make in the name of your Son, and give us the Paraclete whom he promised you would send. May we rejoice always in the presence of your Holy Spirit, and become living signs of his action in the world. We ask this through Christ our Lord. Amen.

—————————— **Day Three** ——————————

# Peace

**Hymn**
*(May be chosen from pp. 48-52)*

**Antiphon**

Come, Holy Spirit, fill the hearts of your faithful, and kindle in them the fire of your love. Send forth your Spirit, and they will be created,

- And you will renew the face of the earth.

**Prayer**

Father of mercy, your Holy Spirit is the sign and instrument of your peace in the world. Fill our hearts with this peace, so that, like St Philip, we may conform our lives to your holy will. We ask this through Christ our Lord. Amen.

**Reading** *(Philippians 4:5b-7,9)*

The Lord is near. Have no anxiety at all, but in everything, by prayer and petition, with thanksgiving, make your requests known to God. Then the peace of God that surpasses all understanding will guard your hearts and minds in Christ Jesus. ... Keep on doing what you have learned and received and heard and seen in me. Then the God of peace will be with you.

**Responsory**                    (cf. *Romans* 5:5; 8:11)

The love of God has been poured into our hearts (alleluia).

- By his Spirit living in us, (alleluia).

## Meditation

"He who wishes for anything but Christ does not know what he wishes; he who asks for anything but Christ does not know what he is asking; he who works, and not for Christ, does not know what he is doing." Such single-mindedness lies at the heart of St Philip's approach to life and ministry, and gives us insight into the source of the peace which pervaded his personality. St Thomas says that the peace that is a fruit of the Holy Spirit involves two things: "freedom from outward disturbance", since our hearts are so fixed on God that they do not attend to external things; and perfect calm, since "our desires rest altogether in one object," namely, doing God's will. St Philip was aware that God required not only all of his love, but also his full attention and complete confidence; because he was able to give them, he enjoyed real peace. "To be entirely conformed and resigned to the divine will is truly a road in which we cannot go wrong, and is the only road which leads us to taste and enjoy that peace which sensual and earthly men know nothing of."

But how does one know that he is truly resigned to the divine will? For St Philip the answer lay in distrusting the self, and putting complete confidence in one's spiritual director. He insisted that the primary relationship in the life of anyone striving for virtue is one of obedience to the spiritual father. "He always asked advice, even on affairs of minor importance. His constant counsel to his penitents was, that they should not trust in themselves, but always take the advice of others, and get as many prayers as they could." "They who really wish to advance in the way of God," he said, "must give themselves up into the hands of their superiors always and in everything. ...There is nothing which gives greater security to our actions, or more effectively cuts the snares the devil lays for us, than to follow another person's will, rather than our own, in doing good."

One anecdote shows how seriously St Philip took his own counsel in regard to obedience. He was on friendly terms with Ignatius of Loyola, who came to visit him often with letters from a fellow Jesuit, Francis Xavier, who was working as a missionary in India and the Far East. As he listened to St Ignatius read these letters, St Philip found himself burning with desire to follow in St Francis's footsteps, and there came a time when he had gathered twenty or so men and was ready to set sail with them for pagan territories. But he would not go until he had consulted a priest whom he had come to trust. This priest told St Philip, "Your Indies are in Rome," and he accepted the advice with peaceful resignation. This conversation took place in

1556; for the next forty years, St Philip worked diligently in Rome and never left the city.

As a spiritual director himself, St Philip often shared this gift of peace with those who turned to him for guidance. Some "recovered their lost peace of mind by simply looking Philip in the face. To dream of him was enough to comfort many. In a word, Philip was a perpetual refreshment to all those who were in perplexity and sadness." Because of this he was in great demand as a counselor and confessor, and his penitents gave him little rest, even when he was sick. But he held nothing back from those who needed to know God's peace; indeed, Newman tells us, "when he was ill, he did not so much receive as impart consolation."

### Litany
(*Optional; may be chosen from pp. 53-60*)
**Our Father, Hail Mary, Glory be.**

### Concluding Prayer
Heavenly Father, hear the prayers that we make in the name of your Son, and give us the Paraclete whom he promised you would send. May the peace that your Holy Spirit brings transform our lives, remove anxiety, and teach us to be obedient to you. We ask this through Christ our Lord. Amen.

———— ✳ ————

# Day Four

# Patience

**Hymn**
(*May be chosen from pp. 48-52*)

**Antiphon**
Come, Holy Spirit, fill the hearts of your faithful, and kindle in them the fire of your love. Send forth your Spirit, and they will be created,
- And you will renew the face of the earth.

**Prayer**
Father, the grace of your Holy Spirit gives us courage to endure all things. Strengthen our hearts, that like St Philip, we may patiently endure every trial, and persevere in doing your will. We ask this through Christ our Lord. Amen.

**Reading** *(James 5:7-8)*
Be patient, therefore, brothers, until the coming of the Lord. See how the farmer waits for the precious fruit of the earth, being patient with it until it receives the early and the late rains. You too must be patient. Make your hearts firm, because the coming of the Lord is at hand.

**Responsory**                    (cf. *Romans* 5:5; 8:11)

The love of God has been poured into our hearts (alleluia).

- By his Spirit living in us, (alleluia).

**Meditation**

The way that St Philip dealt with his own illnesses, which were many, points us to another fruit that the Spirit bore in his life: namely, patience. The Vulgate translation of the Scriptures adds another fruit here, called long-suffering, and St Thomas distinguishes the two in this way: Each, he says, refer to the ability of the mind not to be disturbed. Patience, properly so-called, endures when evil threatens; long-suffering perseveres when good things are delayed. Both aspects of patience were central to St Philip's spirituality. "The great matter," he insisted over and over, "is to persevere."

Certainly patience is necessary in the midst of physical suffering - "Resignation is all in all to the sick man" - but it applies equally to spiritual tribulations, persecutions and misunderstandings as well. St Philip was no stranger to this kind of suffering: on more than one occasion those who misunderstood his efforts or were jealous of his success (often the same people) went out of their way to make life difficult for him, even going so far as to report him to the Holy See as a suspected heretic. Each time he was vindicated and given reassurance, often by the Holy Father himself, but the hurt was real. Still, he saw everything he suffered as part of God's plan, and welcomed it with love. "There is no surer or clearer proof of the love of God than adversity," he advised. "Tribulations, if we bear them patiently for the love of God, appear bitter at first, but they grow sweet when one gets accustomed to the taste."

He likewise advised his penitents to make patience and long-suffering a part of their prayer life: "We must not give up praying because we do not receive what we ask for all at once." Not only did they need to have patience when asking something from God and waiting for it to be fulfilled, but they ought, he said, to make perseverance itself the object of their request. "Among the things we ought to ask of God is perseverance in well-doing and in serving the Lord, because, if we only have patience and persevere in the good life we have begun to lead, we shall acquire a most eminent degree of spirituality. We must often remember what Christ said, that not he who begins, but he who perseveres to the end, shall be saved."

**Litany**
(*Optional; may be chosen from pp. 53-60*)
**Our Father, Hail Mary, Glory be.**

**Concluding Prayer**

Heavenly Father, hear the prayers that we make in the name of your Son, and give us the Paraclete whom he promised you would send. May that Holy Spirit be our strength when we are weak, and help us to bear patiently whatever you ask of us. We ask this through Christ our Lord. Amen.

—————— **Day Five** ——————

# Kindness

**Hymn**
(*May be chosen from pp. 48-52*)

**Antiphon**
Come, Holy Spirit, fill the hearts of your faithful, and kindle in them the fire of your love. Send forth your Spirit, and they will be created,
- And you will renew the face of the earth.

**Prayer**
Merciful Father, your kindness endures forever. May the same Holy Spirit who filled the heart of St Philip fill our hearts also, and make himself known in the kindness we show to those around us. We ask this through Christ our Lord. Amen.

**Reading**                                    (*Ephesians* 4:30-32)
Do not grieve the Spirit of God, with which you have been sealed for the day of redemption. All bitterness, fury, anger, shouting, and reviling must be removed from you, along with all malice. And be kind to one another, compassionate, forgiving one another as God has forgiven you in Christ.

**Responsory**　　　　　　　　　　　(cf. *Romans* 5:5; 8:11)

The love of God has been poured into our hearts (alleluia).

- By his Spirit living in us, (alleluia).

## Meditation

The words that St Thomas uses to discuss the fruit of kindness - also called benignity-are particularly apt in this discussion of the saint with the "heart of fire". Kindness disposes a person to treat other people well, "for the benign are those in whom the salutary flame (*bonus ignis*) of love has enkindled the desire to be kind to their neighbour." The flame of love in St Philip showed itself constantly in the cheerful kindness which he showed to all those around him, so much so that Newman can call him "winning saint" and "sweetest of fathers" without exaggeration. A poem that the Cardinal wrote about his patron has become a favorite hymn of the Oratory, and begins, "This is the saint of gentleness and kindness".

"Cheerfulness strengthens the heart," St Philip says, and so "in dealing with our neighbour we must assume as much pleasantness of manner as we can, and by this affability win him to the ways of virtue." He was convinced that the way to win someone over was by kindness, rather than harshness, and so far this approach seems obvious. He advised priests hearing confessions to be compassionate, and dozens of his penitents bear witness that he followed his own advice. But St Philip's kindness was not affected or insincere; rather, we find its source in his real humility, and in his basic conviction that he was addressing Christ in every person whom he encountered. He was kind to friends and strangers alike: "Philip welcomed those who consulted him with singular benignity, and received them, though strangers, with as much affection as if he had been a long time expecting them."

In dealing with others, benignity requires that we always assume the best of them, and not impute bad motives to the things we see them do. "We should never remind anyone of his natural defects," St Philip counsels, and "we must sometimes bear with little defects in others. We should not be quick at correcting others; we ought to hate no one." Several centuries later, Cardinal Newman would incorporate these and similar sentiments into his definition of a gentleman (in *The Idea of a University*). Kindness is at the heart of the community life that is the essence of the Congregation of the Oratory, and a necessary protection against the dangers that threaten fraternal love. "Our enemy, the devil, who fights with us in order to vanquish us, seeks to disunite us in our houses and to breed quarrels, dislikes, contests, and rivalries... While we are fighting with each other, he comes and conquers us and makes us more securely his own."

But cheerful kindness was not something St Philip advised merely for the sake of winning others. It likewise strengthens the heart of the one who practises it, for by being cheerful we are cooperating with the Spirit of kindness, and allowing the "salutary flame of love" to bear fruit in our actions. "The true way to advance in holy virtues is to persevere in a holy cheerfulness," he says, and "the cheerful are much easier to guide in the spiritual life than the melancholy." The connection between cheerful kindness and growth in spirituality is found in the freedom that comes with humility, and St Philip saw a lack of cheerfulness to be connected with too much self-concern. "Excessive sadness," he insisted, "seldom springs from any other source than pride."

**Litany**
(*Optional; may be chosen from pp. 53-60*)
**Our Father**, **Hail Mary**, **Glory be**.

**Concluding Prayer**
Heavenly Father, hear the prayers that we make in the name of your Son, and give us the Paraclete whom he promised you would send. Set our hearts on fire with your Holy Spirit, and help us to share this flame of love with our brothers and sisters. We ask this through Christ our Lord. Amen.

—————————— **Day Six** ——————————

# Goodness

**Hymn**
(*May be chosen from pp. 48-52*)

**Antiphon**
Come, Holy Spirit, fill the hearts of your faithful, and kindle in them the fire of your love. Send forth your Spirit, and they will be created,
  - And you will renew the face of the earth.

**Prayer**
Loving Father, your generous love overflows in the outpouring of your Holy Spirit. Fill us, as you filled St Philip, with the Spirit of generosity, and teach us to make a gift of ourselves to others. We ask this through Christ our Lord. Amen.

**Reading** (1 *Timothy* 6:18-19)
Tell the rich in the present age not to be proud and not to rely on so uncertain a thing as wealth, but rather on God, who richly provides us with all things for our enjoyment. Tell them to do good, to be rich in good works, to be generous, ready to share, thus accumulating as treasure a good foundation for the future, so as to win the life that is true life.

**Responsory**                          (cf. *Romans* 5:5; 8:11)

The love of God has been poured into our hearts (alleluia).

- By his Spirit living in us, (alleluia).

**Meditation**

Like kindness and cheerfulness, the spiritual fruit of goodness also disposes us well towards our neighbour; here, the Spirit is at work to produce not only good thoughts towards others, but a willingness to do good things for those around us. "Do not let a day pass without doing some good during it," St Philip advised his disciples. "We must not delay in doing good, for death will not delay its time." He felt an urgency about making the love of God and neighbour visible in the form of good works, and this was a watchword with him from the very beginning of his time in Rome. When he met young men on his walks during those early days in Rome, his greeting was always the same: "Well!" he would say, with a grin on his face, "When shall we have a mind to begin to do good?"

This goodness requires a generous spirit, one that is sincerely detached from the world and its material delights. "Give me ten men who are really detached from the world, and wish for nothing but Christ," St Philip once exclaimed, "and I have the heart to believe I could convert the world with them." But the freedom and power that come with detachment are completely squelched by the bonds of avarice. "He who wishes for material possessions will never have devotion. ... He who wishes for perfection must have no attachments to anything of this world." Anecdotes abound of the counsels he gave and the penances he assigned, to gently but firmly lead those who were greedy to renounce their connections to material things.

Generosity for St Philip applied not merely to money and objects - he had few enough of them as it was, and often showed his gratitude for gifts by giving one to the donor that was double the value of the one he had received. More important for him was a commitment to be generous with his time and energy. "If we wish to help our neighbour," he taught, "we must reserve for ourselves neither place, nor hour, nor time." When one of the fathers of the Congregation refused to answer the door to those who came for confession or alms, because he was saying his prayers, St Philip would have none of it. He admonished him and the other fathers and brothers that when they were called for, they were to come immediately, no matter if they were praying or anything else, for in doing so they would be "leaving Christ for Christ."

**Litany**
(*Optional; may be chosen from pp. 53-60*)
**Our Father, Hail Mary, Glory be.**

**Concluding Prayer**
Heavenly Father, hear the prayers that we make in the name of your Son, and give us the Paraclete whom he promised you would send. Let the love of your Holy Spirit abound in our hearts, and help us to bear fruit in good works and generous service to our neighbor. We ask this through Christ our Lord. Amen.

———————— **Day Seven** ————————

# Faithfulness

**Hymn**
(*May be chosen from pp. 48-52*)

**Antiphon**
Come, Holy Spirit, fill the hearts of your faithful, and kindle in them the fire of your love. Send forth your Spirit, and they will be created,
- And you will renew the face of the earth.

**Prayer**
Holy Father, your love for us is everlasting and always true. By the gift of your Holy Spirit keep us faithful to you, that in imitation of St Philip we may serve you with integrity. We ask this through Christ our Lord. Amen.

**Reading**                                    (*Revelation* 2:10b, 25-26)
Remain faithful until death, and I will give you the crown of life... You must hold fast to what you have until I come. To the victor, who keeps my ways until the end, I will give authority over the nations.

**Responsory**                    (cf. *Romans* 5:5; 8:11)

The love of God has been poured into our hearts (alleluia).

- By his Spirit living in us, (alleluia).

## Meditation

St Thomas tells us that the spiritual fruit of fidelity, or faithfulness, has two aspects. On the one hand, fidelity toward our neighbor keeps us from offending him through fraud or deceit. Faithfulness toward God is closely connected with the supernatural virtue of faith, and leads us to subject our intellect, and all that we have, to God. St Philip bore the spiritual fruit of faithfulness equally toward God and his neighbour, providing an example and instruction for his disciples to do the same.

We have seen how gentle and kind St Philip always was toward those around him. He also demanded absolute honesty and integrity in his relationships. "He could not bear two-faced persons," Cardinal Newman tells us, and "as for liars, he could not endure them, and was continually reminding his spiritual children to avoid them as they would a pestilence." Lying to avoid embarrassment was even worse; he insisted that his followers accept the crosses that came to them daily, since "he who runs away from the Cross the Lord sends him" through daily humiliations "will meet a bigger one on the

road." The faithfulness that St Philip practised and
demanded of others was not relaxed in the face of
adversity or hardship. On the contrary, he insisted,
"poverty and tribulations are given us by God as
trials of our fidelity."

St Philip recognised how difficult it is to maintain
this fidelity, especially toward God, in the face of
trials. "Everyone is willing to stand on Mount Tabor
and see Christ transfigured, but few are willing to go
up to Jerusalem and accompany Christ to Mount
Calvary." Therefore he counseled his followers that
the best way to be faithful was to start slowly and
focus on perseverance, rather than try to take on too
much at the beginning, and burn out quickly. "We
must not be too ready to trust young men who have
great devotion," he said, speaking from experience.
"We must wait till their wings are grown and then
see what sort of a flight they make." When someone
came to him full of fire and enthusiasm, he did not
crush their good intentions, but he urged them to
proceed with moderation. "It is well to choose some
one good devotion and stick to it," he advised. "We
must not wish to do everything at once, or become a
saint in four days, but gradually, little by little."

**Litany**
(*Optional; may be chosen from pp. 53-60*)
**Our Father, Hail Mary, Glory be.**

## Concluding Prayer

Heavenly Father, hear the prayers that we make in the name of your Son, and give us the Paraclete whom he promised you would send. Keep us faithful to you, that filled with your grace we may serve and worship you in Spirit and in truth. We ask this through Christ our Lord. Amen.

—————— **Day Eight** ——————

# Gentleness

**Hymn**
(*May be chosen from pp. 48-52*)

**Antiphon**
Come, Holy Spirit, fill the hearts of your faithful, and kindle in them the fire of your love. Send forth your Spirit, and they will be created,
- And you will renew the face of the earth.

**Prayer**
Gentle Father, your justice is revealed in mercy, and your power in forgiveness. May the same Holy Spirit who filled the gentle heart of St Philip, teach us to reach out to others with his tender love. We ask this through Christ our Lord. Amen.

**Reading** (*Ephesians* 4:1-4a)
I, then, a prisoner for the Lord, urge you to live in a manner worthy of the call you have received, with all humility and gentleness, bearing with one another through love, striving to preserve the unity of the spirit through to bond of peace: one body and one Spirit.

**Responsory**                    (cf. *Romans* 5:5; 8:11)

The love of God has been poured into our hearts (alleluia).

- By his Spirit living in us, (alleluia).

## Meditation

Gentleness allows a person to suffer "with equanimity the evils which his neighbour inflicts on him," says St Thomas, and to curb anger. This meekness and gentle spirit was evident in St Philip throughout his life, even when he had become the first Provost or father of the newly-formed Congregation of the Oratory. He did not allow himself to get puffed up with pride because of the authority which he exercised - his advice was that "he who wishes to be perfectly obeyed should give but few orders" - and advised his followers that in all things "a man should keep himself down, and not busy himself *in mirabilibus super* se [in marvels beyond his power]."

St Philip's gentleness allowed him to remain calm even when those around him - sometimes even those closest to him - did not treat him with the respect that he deserved. A famous story is related about Father Talpa, one of the first Oratorians. As Newman tells it, "Once, when he was Superior of the Congregation, one of his subjects snatched a letter out of his hand; but the saint took the affront with incomparable meekness, and neither in look, nor word, nor in gesture betrayed the slightest emotion." Although this may have amazed his other disciples, St Philip demanded that they always follow his example when it came to this kind of mortification. "He who wishes to become a saint must never defend himself. . . . He who cannot put up with the loss of his honour can never advance."

In order to instill this attitude in his disciples, St Philip insisted on the mortification of the *razionale*, the reasoning part of the mind that always wants to have its way, to be given explanations and consulted on matters. To mortify this part of the self was, for St Philip, much more important than external mortifications like fasting, vigils and bodily penances. Whenever someone asked him why his disciples did not fast, "he was accustomed to say, 'The sanctity of a man lies within the space of three fingers,' and, while he said it, he would touch his forehead, and add, in explanation of his words, 'The whole point lies in mortifying the understanding . . . since perfection consists in leading captive our own will and following that of our superiors" (from *The Excellences of the Oratory*).

The penances that St Philip assigned to some of those who came to him for confession are legendary: for example, those who struggled with vanity often found themselves ordered to dress in their best attire and carry St Philip's dog in their arms through the city streets, with a procession of street urchins mocking them all the way. In this manner he hoped to teach his penitents not to be worried about the opinion others had of them, and to "keep down and thwart [that] touchiness of mind" that is a sure sign of pride, and that leads to unkind and ungentle behaviour. Above all else, the struggle to bear the spiritual fruit of meekness and gentleness requires a sense of humour, especially regarding ourselves and our own status. "To persevere in our cheerfulness amid ... troubles is a sign of a right and good spirit."

**Litany**
(*Optional; may be chosen from pp. 53-60*)
**Our Father**, **Hail Mary**, **Glory be**.

**Concluding Prayer**
Heavenly Father, hear the prayers that we make in the name of your Son, and give us the Paraclete whom he promised you would send. May your Holy Spirit teach us to conquer our pride, and to spend our lives in humble, gentle service to our brothers and sisters. We ask this through Christ our Lord. Amen.

———————— Day Nine ————————

# Self-Control

**Hymn**
(*May be chosen from pp. 48-52*)

**Antiphon**
   Come, Holy Spirit, fill the hearts of your faithful, and kindle in them the fire of your love. Send forth your Spirit, and they will be created,
   - And you will renew the face of the earth.

**Prayer**
Father, the wisdom and strength of your Holy Spirit made St Philip a model of chastity to inspire those around him. May that same Spirit strengthen us in mind and body, and teach us to serve you with pure hearts. We ask this through Christ our Lord. Amen.

**Reading**                    (*Galatians* 5:16-17, 24-25)
I say, then: live by the Spirit and you will certainly not gratify the desire of the flesh. For the flesh has desires against the Spirit, and the Spirit against the flesh ...Now those who belong to Christ have crucified their flesh with its passions and desires. If we live in the Spirit, let us also follow the Spirit.

**Responsory**                    (cf. *Romans* 5:5; 8:11)

The love of God has been poured into our hearts (alleluia).

- By his Spirit living in us, (alleluia).

## Meditation

The spiritual fruit of continence, or self-control, is closely connected with the virtue of temperance, and means that the Holy Spirit working in us gives us power to control our bodily desires, and to keep both soul and body in their proper relationship. The Vulgate translation of the letter to the Galatians adds two more spiritual fruits here - modesty and chastity- which further specify the self-control which continence involves, and draw our attention to the importance of integrity and vigilance with regard to sexuality. In St Philip's time, as in our own, chastity was not a "fashionable" virtue, as the art and philosophy of the late Renaissance humanists seemed to revive all of the excesses of ancient paganism. The continence that St Philip displayed in his own life, and encouraged in the lives of others, gives evidence of the power of the Holy Spirit at work in him.

Those who gave testimony during the process of St Philip's canonization noted over and over the great purity which was evident in his whole demeanour - so much so that, as Cardinal Newman tells us, "it shone out of his countenance. His eyes were so clear and bright, even to the last years of his life, that no painter ever succeeded in giving the expression of them... Moreover, his body, even in his old age, emitted a fragrance which refreshed those who came near him." All of his biographers relate that St Philip maintained his virginity throughout his life, despite many attempts by those who were jealous of him to trip him up. His constant approach was to avoid the source of the temptation; he always said that "in the warfare of the flesh, only cowards gain the victory; that is, those who flee."

This was his advice to his penitents as well, for he believed that "in the matter of purity, there is no greater danger than not fearing the danger." "When a person puts himself in the occasion of sin, saying, 'I shall not fall, I shall not commit it,' it is an almost infallible sign that he will fall, and with all the greater damage to his soul." And so he gave his followers some very practical rules for daily living, which were no doubt drawn from years of his own experience: they needed good friends, but should avoid bad company; they were not to retire to their rooms immediately after the mid-day meal; they must avoid idleness. When faced with a sudden temptation, they should fix their minds on something else, no matter what, and use little prayers like "God, come to my assistance. Lord, make haste to help me." Above all, he insisted, frequent use of the Sacrament of

Reconciliation was central to the battle for chastity. "A most excellent means of keeping ourselves pure is to lay open all our thoughts, as soon as possible, to our confessor, with the greatest sincerity, and keep nothing hidden in ourselves. To acquire and preserve the virtue of chastity, we have need of a good and experienced confessor."

This was St Philip's special ministry, and in the confessional he used every gift and fruit of the Spirit to bring souls back to God. It is said that he had a supernatural ability to know who had committed sins against chastity by their smell, and at times he would tell a penitent who was embarrassed and hesitant to confess, "My son, I know your sins already." Notwithstanding his own strict virtue, and this ability to detect the stench of sin, he treated those who came to him to confess sins of impurity with the utmost compassion. "One of the most efficacious means of keeping chaste," he said, "is to have compassion for those who fall through their frailty, and never to boast in the least of being free." He insisted that his disciples treat each other with the same patient understanding, and he used to say that "not to have pity for another in such cases was a forerunner of a speedy fall in ourselves; and that when he found a man censorious, and secure of himself, and without fear, he gave him up for lost."

By his tender guidance St Philip helped many young men to make a good confession and to be set free from years' worth of bad habits and serious sins, and their connection with him enabled them to persevere in chastity. "Many confessed that they were at once delivered from temptations by his merely laying his hands on their heads. The very mention of his name had a power of shielding from Satan those who were assailed by his fiery darts."

**Litany**
(*Optional; may be chosen from pp. 53-60*)
**Our Father, Hail Mary, Glory be.**

**Concluding Prayer**
Heavenly Father, hear the prayers that we make in the name of your Son, and give us the Paraclete whom he promised you would send. May your Holy Spirit cleanse our hearts and strengthen our bodies. May the purity of our lives bear witness to the power of your love. We ask this through Christ our Lord. Amen.

———— �֍ ————

# Hymns

## Come, Holy Ghost

Come Holy Ghost, Creator Blest,
And in our hearts take up Thy rest;
Come with Thy grace and heav'nly aid
To fill the hearts which Thou hast made,
To fill the hearts which Thou hast made.

O Comforter, to Thee we cry,
Thou heav'nly Gift of God most high;
Thou fount of life and fire of love,
And sweet anointing from above,
And sweet anointing from above.

O Holy Ghost, Through thee alone
Know we the Father and the Son;
Be this our firm unchanging creed:
That thou dost from them both proceed,
That thou dost from them both proceed.

Praise be to Thee Father and Son,
And Holy Spirit Three in one;
And may the Son on us bestow
The gifts that from the Spirit flow,
The gifts that from the Spirit flow.

*(Text from the Veni Creator Spiritus. Translated by Fr Edward Caswall of the Oratory.)*

## Veni Creator Spiritus

Come, Holy Spirit,
Creator come,
From your bright
heavenly throne!
Come, take possession
of our souls,
And make them
all your own.

Veni, creátor Spíritus,
mentes tuórum vísita,
imple supérna grátia,
quæ tu creásti péctora.

You who are called
the Paraclete,
Best gift of God above,
The living spring,
the living fire,
Sweet unction,
and true love!

Qui díceris Paráclitus,
altíssimi donum Dei,
fons vivus, ignis, cáritas,
et spiritális únctio.

You who are sevenfold
in your grace,
Finger of God's right hand,
His promise,
teaching little ones
To speak and understand!

Tu septifórmis múnere,
dígitus patérnæ déxteræ,
tu rite promíssum Patris,
sermóne ditans gúttura.

O guide our minds with
your blessed light,

Accénde lumen sénsibus,
infúnde amórem córdibus,

With love our hearts
inflame,
And with your strength
which never decays
Confirm our mortal frame.

infírma nostri córporis
virtúte firmans pérpeti.

Far from us drive our
hellish foe
True peace unto us bring,
And through all perils
guide us safe
Beneath your sacred wing.

Hostem repéllas lóngius
pacémque dones prótinus;
ductóre sic te prǽvio
vitémus omne nóxium.

Through you may we
the Father know,
Through you the eternal
Son
And you the Spirit
of them both
Thrice-blessed three in one.

Per Te sciámus da Patrem
noscámus atque Fílium,
teque utriúsque Spíritum
credámus omni témpore.

All glory to the Father be,
And to the risen Son;
The same to you,
O Paraclete,
While endless ages run.
Amen.

Deo Patri sit glória,
et Fílio, qui a mórtuis
surréxit, ac Paráclito,
in sæculórum sǽcula.

Amen.

*(Attributed to Rabanus Maurus - 766-856.)*

## Hymn to Saint Philip

This is the saint of gentleness and kindness,
Cheerful in penance, and in precept winning;
Patiently healing of their pride and blindness
Souls that are sinning.

This is the saint who, when the world allures us,
Cries her false wares, and ope's her magic coffers,
Points to a better city, and secures us
With richer offers.

Love is his bond; he knows no other fetter,
Asks not our all, but takes whate'er we spare him,
Willing to draw us on from good to better,
As we can bear him.

When he comes near to teach us and to bless us,
Prayer is so sweet that hours are but a minute;
Mirth is so pure, though freely it possess us,
Sin is not in it.

Thus he conducts by holy paths and pleasant
Innocent souls, and sinful souls forgiven,
Towards the bright palace where our God is present,
Throned in high heaven.

This is the saint of gentleness and kindness,
Cheerful in penance, and in precept winning;
Patiently healing of their pride and blindness
Souls that are sinning.

(*John Henry Newman.*)

# Litanies

### Litany of the Holy Spirit

| | |
|---|---|
| Lord, have mercy. | *Lord, have mercy.* |
| Christ, have mercy. | *Christ, have mercy.* |
| Lord, have mercy. | *Lord, have mercy.* |
| Christ, hear us. | *Christ, graciously hear us.* |

God the Father of Heaven,      *Have mercy on us.*
God the Son, Redeemer of the world,
God the Holy Spirit,
Holy Trinity, One God,

Holy Spirit, proceeding from the Father
   and the Son,
Holy Spirit, co-equal with the Father
   and the Son,
Promise of the Father, most bounteous,
Ray of Heavenly Light,
Author of all good,
Source of living Water,
Consuming Fire,
Burning Love,
Spiritual Unction,

Spirit of truth and power,
Spirit of wisdom and understanding,

Spirit of counsel and fortitude,
Spirit of knowledge and piety,
Spirit of fear of the Lord,
Spirit of compunction,
Spirit of grace and prayer,
Spirit of love, peace and joy,
Spirit of patience,
Spirit of longanimity and goodness,
Spirit of benignity and mildness,
Spirit of fidelity,
Spirit of modesty and continence,
Spirit of chastity,
Spirit of adoption of sons of God,

Holy Spirit, our Comforter,
Holy Spirit, our Sanctifier,
You Who in the beginning moved upon the
    waters,
You through Whom spoke holy men of God,
You Who overshadowed the Virgin Mary,
You by Whom Mary conceived Christ,
You Who descend upon men at Baptism,
You Who, on the Day of Pentecost appeared
    through fiery tongues,
You by Whom we are reborn,
You Who dwell in us as in a Temple,
You Who govern and animate the Church,
You Who fill the whole world,

That You will renew the face of the earth,
*We beseech You, hear us.*
That You may shed Your Light upon us,
That You may pour Your Love into our hearts,
That You may inspire us to love our neighbour,
That You may teach us to ask for the graces we
    need,
That You may enlighten us with your heavenly
    inspirations,
That You may guide us in the way of holiness,
That You may make us obedient to Your
    commandments,
That You may teach us how to pray,
That You may always pray with us,
That You may inspire us with horror for sin,
That You may direct us in the practice of virtue,
That You may make us persevere in a holy life,
That You may make us faithful to our vocation,
That You may grant us good priests and bishops,
That You may give us good Christian families,
That You may grant us a spiritual renewal of the
    Church,
That You may guide and console the Holy Father,

Lamb of God, who takes away the sins of
    the world:
*Spare us, O Lord.*

Lamb of God, who takes away the sins of the
   world:
*Graciously hear us, O Lord.*
Lamb of God, who takes away the sins of the world:
*Have mercy on us.*
Holy Spirit, hear us.
*Holy Spirit, Graciously hear us.*

Lord, have mercy.                *Lord, have mercy.*
Christ, have mercy.              *Christ, have mercy.*
Lord, have mercy.                *Lord, have mercy.*

Create a clean heart in us, O Lord.
*Renew a right spirit in us, O Lord.*

Let us pray:
O God, who enlightens the hearts of the faithful
by the light of the Holy Spirit, grant to us the same
Spirit, that we may be truly wiseand ever rejoice in
his consolation.We ask this through Christ our
Lord. Amen.

### The Litany of St Philip

| | |
|---|---|
| Lord, have mercy | *Lord, have mercy.* |
| Christ, have mercy | *Christ, have mercy.* |
| Lord, have mercy | *Lord, have mercy.* |
| Christ, hear us | *Christ, graciously hear us.* |

| | |
|---|---|
| God the Father of heaven | *Have mercy on us.* |
| God the Son, Redeemer of the World, | *Have mercy on us.* |
| God the Holy Ghost, | *Have mercy on us.* |
| Holy Trinity, One God, | *Have mercy on us.* |

| | |
|---|---|
| Holy Mary, | *Pray for us.* |
| Holy Mother of God, | *Pray for us.* |
| Holy Virgin of Virgins, | *Pray for us.* |

| | |
|---|---|
| St Philip, | *Pray for us.* |
| Vessel of the Holy Ghost, | *Pray for us.* |
| Child of Mary, | *Pray for us.* |
| Apostle of Rome, | *Pray for us.* |
| Counsellor of Popes, | *Pray for us.* |
| Voice of prophecy, | *Pray for us.* |
| Man of primitive times, | *Pray for us.* |
| Winning saint, | *Pray for us.* |
| Hidden hero, | *Pray for us.* |
| Sweetest of Fathers, | *Pray for us.* |
| Flower of purity, | *Pray for us.* |
| Martyr of charity, | *Pray for us.* |

Heart of fire,                          *Pray for us.*
Discerner of spirits,                   *Pray for us.*
Choicest of priests,                    *Pray for us.*
Mirror of the divine life,              *Pray for us.*
Pattern of humility,                    *Pray for us.*
Example of simplicity,                  *Pray for us.*
Light of holy joy,                      *Pray for us.*
Image of childhood,                     *Pray for us.*
Picture of old age,                     *Pray for us.*
Director of souls,                      *Pray for us.*
Gentle guide of youth,                  *Pray for us.*
Patron of thine own,                    *Pray for us.*

Who didst observe chastity in thy youth,
*Pray for us.*
Who didst seek Rome by divine guidance,
*Pray for us.*
Who didst hide so long in the Catacombs,
*Pray for us.*
Who didst receive the Holy Ghost into thy heart,
*Pray for us.*
Who didst experience such wonderful exstacies,
*Pray for us.*
Who didst so lovingly serve the little ones,
*Pray for us.*
Who didst wash the feet of pilgrims,
*Pray for us.*

Who didst ardently thirst after martyrdom,
*Pray for us.*
Who didst distribute the daily word of God,
*Pray for us.*
Who didst turn so many hearts to God,
*Pray for us.*
Who didst converse so sweetly with Mary,
*Pray for us.*
Who didst raise the dead,
*Pray for us.*
Who didst set up thy houses in all lands,
*Pray for us.*

Lamb of God, who takest away the sins of the world,
*Spare us, O Lord.*
Lamb of God, who takest away the sins of the world,
*Graciously hear us, O Lord.*
Lamb of God, who takest away the sins of the world,
*Have mercy on us.*
Christ, hear us
*Christ, graciously hear us.*

V. Remember thy Congregation,
R. Which thou hast possessed from the beginning.

Let us pray:
O God, who hast exalted blessed Philip, thy
Confessor, in the glory of thy saints, grant that, as we
rejoice in his commemoration, so we may profit by
the example of his virtues, through Christ our Lord.

**R.** Amen.

# Philip Neri

*CTS Great Saints Series*

**The Light of Holy Joy**

This new and innovative retelling of the life of one of Europe's favourite saints, uses Newman's Litany of St Philip Neri to shed light on the many facets of the founder of the Oratorians. His great holiness, influence on the Church and sense of fun are simply presented to give a great introduction to the life of the Apostle of Rome.

ISBN 1 86082 171 5
CTS Code: B670

*Compendium*

# CATECHISM OF THE CATHOLIC CHURCH

"The *Compendium*, which I now present to the Universal Church, is a faithful and sure synthesis of the *Catechism of the Catholic Church*. It contains, in concise form, all the essential and fundamental elements of the Church's faith, thus constituting, as my Predecessor had wished, a kind of *vademecum*, which allows believers and non-believers alike to behold the entire panorama of the Catholic faith.".

*Benedictus PP XVI*

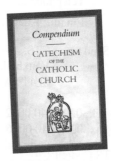

ISBN 1 86082 376 9
CTS Code: Do 742

# Informative Catholic Reading

We hope that you have enjoyed reading this booklet.

If you would like to find out more about CTS booklets - we'll send you our free information pack and catalogue.

Please send us your details:

Name .............................................................

Address .........................................................

.......................................................................

.......................................................................

Postcode .......................................................

Telephone......................................................

Email .............................................................

Send to:    CTS, 40-46 Harleyford Road,
             Vauxhall, London
             SE11 5AY

Tel: 020 7640 0042
Fax: 020 7640 0046
Email: info@cts-online.org.uk